FORGIVENESS

FINDING FREEDOM FROM YOUR PAST

HARVEY R. BROWN, JR.

Energion Publications
Gonzalez, FL
2013

THE UNIVERSAL QUEST

You have made us for yourself,
and our heart is restless until it finds rest in you.

— Augustine

The stench is every bit as thick as the sea of humanity that huddles en masse along the banks of the river. A soup of sun-cooked mud and human dung oozes between pilgrim toes as they push their way into polluted waters. But the filth beneath their feet is nothing compared to the soul-stain that drives them to come to Allahabad year after year. The Ganges River in North India is thought to be a goddess. For the people along the water's edge—literally tens of millions of them—the river holds hope that a ritual bath in her waters will somehow cleanse them of sin and release them from an endless cycle of reincarnation.

In the Philippines, barefoot penitents flog themselves with lead-tipped whips, and two dozen or so have themselves nailed to crosses in a series of crucifixions on an artificial hill. The decades old practice, which became established in the province as a form of religious vow to merit God's forgiveness, annually draws thousands of curiosity seekers from around the world.

A famous American talk show personality with her own TV network has a "spirit" section as the focus of her immensely popular web site. Over a hundred million unique visitors find the latest new-age gurus offering advice on breaking free from guilt—including instructions on how to atone for your failures by learning "how to consciously make a sacrifice in light of your desire for forgiveness."[1]

---

1 http://www.oprah.com/oprahs-lifeclass/Rituals-for-Forgiveness/
   2#ixzz2ghFhGNPE

A missionary in South Asia walks along the road on the outskirts of a city of nine million people. A young man named Srinu comes up beside him and asks if the American is a Christian. The answer is yes. When the missionary asks if he has a spiritual belief, the young man tells him all the things he is doing as a Hindu—going to the temple, offering sacrifices, helping needy people and being baptized. "How many of those things must you do to have your sins forgiven?" asks the missionary.

"I do not know."[2]

SOMETHING'S BROKEN

We may not know the answer to the missionary's question either. But we do know that deep inside our hearts is an unmet need.

Within every person—regardless of culture, race, or background—is an innate awareness that something about themselves is profoundly flawed or greatly broken. "Human need and human sin are not geographical … in a round world it is difficult to tell where East begins and West ends. We are *all* in the same deep need."[3]

That *deep need* is the need to receive forgiveness for our sins.

The four examples at the beginning of this chapter underscore the universal recognition of sin's presence. The question is not *does sin exist*. The real question is *how do you deal with sin and obtain true and lasting forgiveness*. How do you find freedom from your past?

That's what this little book is all about. In the following pages, we are going to look together at the nature of sin—and the nature of lasting forgiveness. It comes through our relationship with Jesus Christ because of God's love.

---

2   http://www.pastornotes.com/tracts/need_sins_forgiven.pdf

3   E. Stanley Jones, Sermon entitled, The Seditious Sermon, http://www.ephrataministries.org/remnant-2011-01-seditious-sermon.a5w

FORGIVENESS IS GOD'S IDEA

To err is human; to forgive, divine. — Alexander Pope

Forgiveness is the foundation of the gospel (good news). Jesus came so we could receive forgiveness of our sins, so we could be brought into God's forever family, so that we might discover our destiny as sons and daughters of the Creator of the Universe.

When people discuss the nature of God, they frequently use three rather large words to describe his attributes. They say God is omniscient, omnipresent, and omnipotent. Each word begins with the Latin prefix "omni," meaning "all." So *omniscient* means he is all knowing, *omnipresent* means that he is everywhere—there is nowhere he is not, and *omnipotent* means he is all powerful.

If God really is all knowing, he obviously knows everything before it happens. He has advance knowledge of every occurrence in human history. Even before Creation, God has known what will transpire. Has it ever occurred to you that *nothing* has ever occurred to God?[4]

Never surprised. Never caught flat-footed. Never scrambling for solutions to new problems that sneaked up on him. That means that God has always been aware of our need for a solution to the problem of sin, guilt, and forgiveness—even all the way back to the Garden of Eden.

THE COVER-UP

The first three chapters in the Bible are the account of God creating everything in the natural world around us. The final, crowning act of creation was when he made man. Most of Genesis 2 tells the story:

> Then the Lord God formed the man from the dust of the ground. He breathed the breath of life into the man's nostrils,

---

4   Dr. Jack R. Taylor, in a sermon delivered in Jefferson City, Tennessee, August 24, 2013.

and the man became a living person. Then the Lord God planted a garden in Eden in the east, and there he placed the man he had made. The Lord God made all sorts of trees grow up from the ground—trees that were beautiful and that produced delicious fruit. In the middle of the garden he placed the tree of life and the tree of the knowledge of good and evil …. The Lord God placed the man in the Garden of Eden to tend and watch over it. But the Lord God warned him, "You may freely eat the fruit of every tree in the garden—except the tree of the knowledge of good and evil. If you eat its fruit, you are sure to die." … Now the man and his wife were both naked, but they felt no shame.[5]

Things in the Garden were going splendidly for Adam and Eve. That is until …

The serpent was the shrewdest of all the wild animals the Lord God had made. One day he asked the woman, "Did God really say you must not eat the fruit from any of the trees in the garden?"

"Of course we may eat fruit from the trees in the garden," the woman replied. "It's only the fruit from the tree in the middle of the garden that we are not allowed to eat. God said, 'You must not eat it or even touch it; if you do, you will die.'"

"You won't die!" the serpent replied to the woman. "God knows that your eyes will be opened as soon as you eat it, and you will be like God, knowing both good and evil."

The woman was convinced. She saw that the tree was beautiful and its fruit looked delicious, and she wanted the wisdom it would give her. So she took some of the fruit and ate it. Then she gave some to her husband, who was with her, and he ate it, too.[6]

Eve was deceived by the lies of the serpent—utterly convinced that it was a good thing to eat the fruit. After she ate, she gave

---

5 Genesis 2:7-9, 15-17, 25 (NLT)
6 Genesis 3:1–6 (NLT)

some to her husband. There is no indication in the text that Adam believed the lie. Since the Bible says that he was with her, we can reasonably assume that he heard the whole conversation—and did nothing to intervene in the deception. He just took what Eve gave him and ate.

Adam's disobedience was willful independence from God. He heard directly from God that he was not to eat the fruit. But Eve didn't. Not yet created when God told Adam to stay away from the tree, there is no record that she had heard these words from God himself. Eve was fooled. Adam was without excuse.

As a result of their sin, Adam and Eve realized they were na-ked—exposed—and conceived a plan to cover themselves. They stitched fig leaves together for garments to hide their nakedness.

It doesn't take very long for leaves to become dry and brittle after they are picked. The latest fashion (actually, the very first) hardly made it from designer to model before it began to unravel and fall apart. So Adam and Eve hid from God when they heard him taking his evening walk in the Garden.

The account of God's confrontation with Adam, Eve, and the serpent is recorded in the latter parts of Genesis 3. After telling them the results of their sin and its long-term effects, God himself took the initiative to cover their exposure with something far better than fig leaves. God made garments of animal skin and clothed them.

Consider this: In order for garments to be made of animal skin, an animal has to die. The life of a creature had to be sacrificed to cover the sin of another creature. This act of sacrifice mirrors Jesus' own sacrifice on the cross, dying to cover our sins. As the writer of Hebrews puts it, "... without the shedding of blood there is no forgiveness."[7]

In the Old Testament, the Bible details very precise rituals that Hebrews observed for offering sacrifices to atone for their sins. Based on God's instructions, they performed sacrifices for sins of

---

7   Hebrews 9:22b (NIV84)

varying kinds and degrees. There was an annual Day of Atonement when the priests offered sacrifice to atone for the sins of the nation. The repetition of these sacrifices, though, shows that they were never sufficient to cleanse persons permanently of their sin. "Therefore no one will be declared righteous in God's sight by the works of the law; rather, through the law we become conscious of our sin."[8] That includes all the sacrifices prescribed in the law, even if they were for atonement.

There was one special religious festival that God placed among the various ceremonial laws. It foreshadowed his plan to cover forever the sins of all. The Jews knew it as Passover.

Passover was an annual reminder to the Israelites of their deliverance from slavery in Egypt. On the night before Pharaoh let them go, God sent the angel of death to kill all Egyptian first born, both human and animal. In order for the angel to distinguish the homes of the Israelites from the Egyptians, the Jews were instructed to kill a lamb—one with no defects in form or appearance—and smear some blood over the doorways of their homes. When the Death Angel saw the blood above the doors, it passed over the houses where the Jews lived and they were spared the plague that devastated the Egyptians.

ANOTHER LAMB

When Jesus first appears as an adult in the pages of the New Testament, he is going to John the Baptist to be baptized. Upon seeing him, John declares, "Look, the Lamb of God, who takes away the sin of the world!"[9]

Christians who study the Bible have come to understand that much of what happened in the Old Testament is used by God to foreshadow (picture ahead of time) things that are revealed in the New Testament. The role of the Passover lamb—a picture of what Jesus did for us on the cross—is example of this. John the

8   Romans 3:20 (NIV)
9   John 1:29 (NIV84)

6

Baptist's statement repaints that picture in the most vivid of hues. What was previously shadowed is now boldly proclaimed.

John, as a prophet, saw Jesus as the coming sacrifice whose blood would cover, once and for all, the sin of humanity. No longer is Jesus just the babe in the manger who would save the people from their sins. He now is plainly revealed as the Lamb—the ultimate Passover lamb—who would die to cover sin with *his own blood.*

With full knowledge of mankind's coming sin, this pre-existent God—Father, Son, and Holy Spirit—determined before Creation to do for us what we could never do for ourselves. In Heaven the decision was made. Divine, self-giving love would provide the necessary atonement (covering) true forgiveness requires. Jesus, the Son of God, would come to Earth as a man, live a sinless life, and as a perfect (flawless) sacrifice offer himself for the sin of all. "The death of Jesus Christ is the performance in history of the very mind of God … His death was the very reason why He came."[10]

BREAKING DOWN THE BARRIER

The Bible teaches that because we are directly descended from Adam, sin is an inborn spiritual defect inherited by every one of us. This genetic predisposition toward sin has the same effect on our relationship with God as did Adam's. We too attempt to hide.

Adam and Eve used fig leaves to try to conceal their failure, but most of us hide behind lies. To cover our sin and its consequences, we stitch together flimsy excuses and decorate them with ornate stories trying to keep others from discovering who we really are or how badly we have failed. The further we go, the more creative our lies must become to keep our secrets hidden. Brick-by-brick we build barriers to hide behind hoping that the real truth about our sin and brokenness is never revealed.

Or we sequester parts of our lives into locked-away compartments. This compartmentalization allows our subconscious to avoid

10 Oswald Chambers, *My Utmost For His Highest*, http://utmost.org/it-is-finished/

the discomfort caused by having conflicting values, emotions, or behaviors within ourselves. Hiding these sin-tainted images in the dark corners of our memories, we try to convince ourselves that we are really doing OK. Although this process attempts to isolate areas of failure in our minds, ultimately we discover that not acknowledging them will never eradicate their presence. We still need help beyond ourselves.

No matter how we try to deal with our own "stuff," the aggressive mercy of God relentlessly pursues us. By his grace he continues to press in beyond our excuses and hiding—first convicting us of our sin and then leading us to the cross. Here we discover grace and help in time of need. God pursues us and does not let us rest until we find our rest in him. When we surrender to his insistent love, we run into the everlasting arms of the One from whom we hid. He has destroyed every barrier that separated us from himself and opened the door to forgiveness that no one can shut. We then can freely respond to his love as one of his dear children. "Because of Christ and our faith in him, we can now come boldly and confidently into God's presence."[11]

A well-worn expression says, "I'll believe it when I see it." But for me, I didn't *see* it until I believed it. Let me tell you what I mean.

---

11 Ephesians 3:12 (NLT)

Believing Is Seeing

*It's impossible to please God apart from faith. And why?
Because anyone who wants to approach God must believe both
that he exists and that he cares enough to respond to those who
seek him.*[12]

My sister, older by two-and-a-half years, was a student at the
University of Georgia. Once I had my driver's license, I began
making weekend pilgrimages to see her. Sis would get me dates
with girls from the local high school, and I would attend fraternity
parties as the guest of guys who wanted to stay in her good graces.
I was big stuff in my adolescent mind, far above the juvenile high-
school scene: I was a collegian-in-waiting, just marking time at
home until I could be a real Georgia Bulldog.

To fulfill my dream as soon as possible, I enrolled in the university one week after high school graduation. I got a head start
on my college career by attending summer school. What could
possibly be better than attending Georgia football games with a
co-ed on my arm and a fraternity pledge pin on my chest? Only
becoming a BMOC—big man on campus.

It seemed that everything I thought I wanted or needed to
be "somebody" on campus came my way. Outwardly, everything
looked great. I was president of my fraternity pledge class and
elected an officer the day after I was initiated. I was "cool" because
I worked in an exclusive men's store near campus. It was an extro-
vert's heaven: twenty-thousand students, and I was running with
the best. Student government-appointed positions, my photograph
plastered throughout the university yearbook, and the academic
honors program were to come during the next three years.

But no matter how much recognition I achieved or how many
goals I reached, inside I felt hopeless and worthless. I had terribly
low self-esteem buried beneath my confident and cocky exterior.

---

12 Hebrews 11:6 (The Message)

On the outside I was Joe Cool, BMOC, Frat Man. On the inside I was a nobody—insecure and always looking for some way to prop myself up emotionally. Nothing seemed to satisfy the soul-deep emptiness I felt.

By my senior year, my collegiate dream had become a nightmare. The party was now a wake. I lived a life of spiritual and moral death where college was no longer a blast, even though I was more frequently "getting blasted." With my hedonism rushing me headlong towards hell, I sat in my apartment one night with my hands over my face.

Why not just end it all? I reasoned. Self-destructive thoughts were common as my depression deepened. I was now recycling the idea of suicide. A litany of supposed successes paraded before me and, like the child declaring that the emperor had no clothes, mocked the emptiness of all the things I once considered so important.

Looking for fraternity brotherhood, instead I had found a drinking club. My arrogance—worn to cover my minimal self-esteem—so alienated me from my brothers that I eventually became an inactive member. *They're losers,* I told myself, while really feeling deep in my heart that I was the real loser.

I sought consolation in a relationship with a young lady who was one of the prettiest girls on campus, but like so many other things she was just a prop. I assumed people seeing us together would respect me, but my dour outlook and self-absorption eventually pushed her away. She broke up with me. Now all I had left was lingering pain as a memory of our time together.

In my depression I stopped attending classes, instead hanging out at the Student Center's Bulldog Room—smoking, joking, playing bridge, and pretending to be the life of the party. During these times I was able to forget my feelings, if just for a little while. My grades had taken a nose dive. There I was, a zoology major and member of international premedical honor society, about to make a D, F, and WF (Withdrew, Failing) in three five-hour major subjects.

No wonder suicide had become a recurring thought. Whenever I returned to my apartment and was alone, I had to confront the emptiness of my life. Everything that I thought would make me happy had failed to fulfill.

The box of barbiturates was still there in the drawer. Wash the pills down with the rest of the whiskey in the bottle on the shelf, go to sleep, and say, "To hell with this world." That seemed like the only alternative to the pain I felt in my soul. But I needed to do one final thing.

If I were going to have one last shot at making an impression, I wanted to make sure that it was done right. Why not plan the funeral? My yearbook photo was great. I was the ultimate preppie in my bow tie and vested suit. I could see it in the hometown paper—obituary with photo, the list of honors and activities. Everyone would wonder why. The burden of achievement? The pressure of being so successful? I would take the secret to my grave: I would kill myself because I was lost and lonely.

The plans for the funeral unfolded rapidly before me: Solid walnut casket, no tacky praying hands, a casket spray of white carnations (my fraternity flower). My fraternity brothers would be honorary pall bearers. In my mind's eye I could see the cortege winding its way up the paths of Rose Hill Cemetery. Believing that image was everything, I continued to ponder my grand exit.

But when I finished, sitting in an old overstuffed chair and feeling a macabre satisfaction over the details, a voice spoke to me. It uttered only three words. Whether the voice was heard by my ears or my mind, it hit me just the same:

"Who will mourn?"

"What do you mean, *Who will mourn?*" I said aloud.

My mind raced to review those who would attend my funeral. My parents would mourn. My sister would mourn. But my fraternity would probably use the funeral as an excuse for an out-of-town

11

party. Political figures would show up, but only because my dad was a lobbyist. The more I thought, the more I realized that my life had absolutely no impact beyond the immediate family circle. Here I was about to make my last big splash, but it looked to be more of a ripple.

My emotions ebbed even further. I had worked so long to create an image, yet the final sculpture was nothing but clay. It would not last. It could not last.

I finally came to a decision: There would be no suicide tonight. No, there must be some way to pull this thing together. Who could I talk with? Where could I find help?

Just two weeks before, my friend Toby and I had been on our way to play golf when two sharp-looking guys struck up a conversation with us in the parking lot. Since we had been in a hurry to leave, we said we would meet them for dinner later that night.

Dave Wilcoxon and Ron Kyzer were not much older than we, but they certainly seemed to have their acts together. It turned out that they were staff members of Campus Crusade for Christ, a Christian ministry that focused on college students. As we were eating our meal, they shared about knowing Jesus. *Fanatics,* I remembered thinking.

After listening to what they had to say, I was still convinced that my lifestyle and ethical decision-making process was exemplary. Those honors philosophy courses weren't lost on me.

"Well, I understand your religious interest," I said, "but I'm perfectly OK without all that stuff. Everybody has the right to believe what they choose. I'm just not where you guys are. But," I added, "I respect what you stand for."

I felt like I dismissed their challenge rather easily. The meal was enjoyable, but I didn't need what they were offering. I had joined a church as a young teen. I knew the Christmas and Easter stories. I believed God existed. But all this talk of knowing Him in a real way made me uncomfortable.

As we parted after dinner that night, Ron smiled and waved. "Remember guys, if you ever want to talk any more, I'm the last 'K' in the phone book."

Don't hold your breath, I thought.

As the ticking of the wind-up alarm clock counted off sleepless moments of a never-ending night, I grew even more despondent. Almost without thinking I picked up the phonebook, turned to the right section, and found Ron Kyzer's name where he had said it would be. You just couldn't get any more last than having a "y" and "z" in your name.

At 1:35 a.m. I dialed his phone number.

Fifteen minutes later Ron was knocking on my apartment door. When I let him in, he squeezed my shoulder and looked me in the eye. His coming let me know he really cared.

I blurted out all of my frustrations and dashed dreams. I described in detail—and very colorful language—my sense of hopelessness. Throughout everything, Ron listened carefully.

"Harvey, I'm not exactly sure how to respond. Do you mind if we pray together before I share anything?"

I nodded, feeling detached from what he was saying.

After he prayed, Ron took out a small paper-backed Bible, turned a few pages, then underlined some words. He handed it to me so that I could read what he had underlined.

> *If we say that we have no sin, we deceive ourselves, and there is no truth in us. But if we confess our sins to God, he will keep his promise and do what is right: he will forgive us our sins and purify us from all our wrongdoing.*[13]

That was it. That was it!

In an instant I had illumination rather than human understanding. The moment I finished reading the last word I knew

---

13 1 John 1:8-9 (GNT)

in my heart exactly what the issue was. *Sin*—my sin! That's what separated me from God.

Even though I gave no intellectual assent to the concept of sin, sin nonetheless was controlling my life and killing me. But the Holy Spirit was leading me into all truth. He showed me through Ron's choice of scripture (1 John 1:8-9) that the remedy for sin was Jesus. I felt like a cartoon character with a light bulb drawn above his head. I suddenly understood.

I looked up at Ron. "What do I do?"

"Talk to God, just like I'm talking to you. He's not as concerned with your words as He is with the attitude of your heart." Then he paused. "If you'd like, Harvey, we can pray together—you take my words and make them your words. God will hear."

Ron closed his eyes and started to pray. Out loud, phrase-by-phrase, I began repeating every word he said.

> *Lord Jesus, I need You. Thank You for dying on the cross for my sins. I open the door of my life and receive You as my Savior and Lord.*

When I asked Jesus to come into my life, it was like my gut, which had been tied in knots for so long, suddenly untied. I literally could feel the release.

Then I asked Him to forgive my sins.

> *Thank You for forgiving my sins and giving me eternal life.*

At that moment I felt as if someone lifted a backpack full of rocks from my shoulders. The weight of the burden of my sin was gone. I knew—positively knew—that *my* sins were forgiven.

> *Take control of the throne of my life. Make me the kind of person You want me to be. Amen.*

That was it. Simple. To the point. Life changing. Now I belonged to Jesus.

I was born again.[14]

14 Portions of this chapter have been excerpted from the author's book
*When God Strikes The Match: Igniting A Passion For Holiness
And Renewal*, Revival Press (an imprint of Destiny Image), 1997,
Shippensburg, PA.

STEPS TO RECEIVING FORGIVENESS

There is no limit to God's grace in accepting our failures.
                                                    – Phillip Yancey

Different people process information differently. Intuitive types may gravitate toward ideas and concepts because of an ability to "connect the dots" without needing to have a lot of detail. Sensory types may process information in a more linear, step-by-step fashion and prefer to have every part of the process spelled out clearly. Regardless of your preferred style for processing information, the following is critically important in dealing with forgiveness.

Jesus Christ's death upon the cross was sufficient in satisfying God's righteous requirements to forgive. When Jesus cried out, "It is finished,"[15] everything that was necessary to be done had been done. All was accomplished. It *was* finished ... at least God's part.

In the transaction required to have our sins forgiven, there are two parties involved—the one who has sinned, and God, the one who forgives. Our sins may have social consequences such as damaged relationships, sexually transmitted diseases, broken laws, or physical harm. But when we become aware of our sins before God, we begin to realize the weight of our offenses extends far beyond social consequences. We begin to see our sinfulness in light of his holiness. Our hearts are like those of King David when he wrote, "For I know my transgressions, and my sin is always before me. Against you, you only, have I sinned and done what is evil in your sight, ..."[16]

This overwhelming conviction of sin is a gift from God that draws us toward the Author of life and mercy. "For the kind of sorrow God wants us to experience leads us away from sin and

---

15 John 19:30
16 Psalm 51:3-4a (NIV84)

results in salvation. There's no regret for that kind of sorrow. But worldly sorrow, which lacks repentance, results in spiritual death."[17]

The key word in the last sentence is *repentance*—which literally means "turning around." The conscious decision to turn from our sin and turn to God for forgiveness is *our* part in this two-part transaction. When we repent, our acceptance of God's free gift of forgiveness through Christ actualizes forgiveness for each of us.

A simple illustration will help us see this in a different light.

Imagine that unknown to you, someone had opened a checking account in your name at a local bank. At the time they opened it, they linked your account to their own through an unlimited line of credit. There is no possibility of overdraft. Funds would always be available regardless of the size of the demand put on the account.

So far there's only one problem. You don't know about the account and how to access it. All you have been doing is running up debts that you can't pay.

The bank account is a picture of what God has done for us through supplying the gift of forgiveness. By his own initiative he already made provision for everything that is needed—as well as covering anything that ever would be needed.

I remember when we opened a new bank account after we moved to our current location. One of the requirements was for us, as account holders, to sign the signature cards. This indicated that we had entered into a contract with the bank to use the account according to bank regulations. Only then were we given access to all the funds deposited in the account.

Knowing that you are a sinner—and that God has made provision for covering your sin—is not enough. You need to "sign the card" by repenting, by turning from your sin and your own efforts to deal with it, and simply *ask* God to forgive you.

Repentance is so much more than being sorry. It is a decision. Once you repent, you receive the full measure of God's forgiveness. Your acceptance of God's provision through the death of Jesus on

---

17 2 Corinthians 7:10 (NLT)

the cross allows you to draw from his limitless supply. Regardless of the enormity of the debt, God's grace is sufficient to cover *every* sin—and *all* sin. You draw from his resources and find grace and help in time of need.

As you read this, you might be saying, "I think I need to do that." The choice is up to you. Even if you have previously drawn from God's limitless supply of forgiveness, if there is something you need to take care of, stop and do it. You can repent and ask for forgiveness right here, right now. Here is a prayer you can pray:

> *Father, I know I am a sinner. I need your forgiveness. In the name of Jesus, I repent of my sin and turn to you. Forgive all my sin. Tear down every barrier I have erected between us. Thank you for forgiving me, cleansing me, and accepting me. In Jesus' name, Amen.*

A HEART TO FORGIVE

*Forgive all who have offended you, not for them, but for
yourself.* — Harriet Nelson

"I'd rather go to hell than to heaven if there's a chance *he*
would be there."

Never in my young pastoral life had I heard someone utter
words that were—at least to my mind—unspeakable for any person
who supposedly was a Christian. I tried not to let my face show how
stunned I was at the woman's remark. The intensity of the anger and
pain I was seeing was scary. *This was just supposed to be a visit to an
inactive church member,* I thought. *What have I gotten myself into?*

Some members had told me of a woman who dropped out
of church. My bishop had recently appointed me to pastor a little
country church where Mrs. Willoughby had once attended. She
had been the Sunday School superintendent, women's mission society president, and a faithful participant in all its activities. Yet
something had derailed her faith life, and for the last few years
she had closed herself off from friends and fellowship at Thomas
Chapel United Methodist Church.

Mrs. Willoughby was cordial and welcomed me into her
home. After a few minutes of introductory conversation, I moved
right to the point of my visit. "Your friends told me about your
previous involvement in the church, and I was curious why you
were no longer coming."

"I don't want to go to church anymore," she replied curtly.
"My life has been ruined because of that man and what he did to
my granddaughter." She then began to spew out a story of disappointment, anguish, distress ... and hatred toward the man who
"stole her baby."

Mrs. Willoughby had been raising the child. Once the girl was
in high school and old enough to work, she got an after school job
as cashier at the grocery store in their little community. The young

woman earned praise from her boss, who over time began to lavish extra attention on the emotionally needy girl. Before the school year was over, she and her boss had run away together. The boss left his wife, family, and job. The girl left her grandmother—never to be seen again.

The girl was gone for good. In her place, unforgiveness and bitterness moved into the grandmother's heart.

ENTER THE TORMENTORS

On one occasion, Peter—a disciple of Jesus—asked his Master a question regarding forgiveness. "Lord, how often should I forgive someone who sins against me? Seven times?"[18]

Jesus' answer elevated the issue of how we forgive others far beyond anything Peter could have imagined. "No, not seven times," Jesus replied, "but seventy times seven."[19]

When you do the math, you realize that Jesus' answer was staggering compared to Peter's expectation. Four hundred ninety is so much greater than the seven times Peter thought would get the Lord's approval. If I were among those who heard Jesus' response, I would have blurted out, "Lord, that's impossible!"

But this is just the kind of response Jesus intended to evoke. He was telling Peter (and all of us who are listening through the pages of scripture) that there is no way humanly possible to implement such a standard of forgiveness—certainly not in our own strength. There is hope for us, however. This is the same Jesus who said, "Humanly speaking, it is impossible. But with God everything is possible."[20]

Peter's question about forgiveness set the stage for a story Jesus told.

18 Matthew 18:21 (NLT)
19 Matthew 18:22 (NLT)
20 Matthew 19:26 (NLT)

Therefore, the Kingdom of Heaven can be compared to a king who decided to bring his accounts up to date with servants who had borrowed money from him. In the process, one of his debtors was brought in who owed him millions of dollars. He couldn't pay, so his master ordered that he be sold—along with his wife, his children, and everything he owned—to pay the debt.

But the man fell down before his master and begged him, "Please, be patient with me, and I will pay it all." Then his master was filled with pity for him, and he released him and forgave his debt.

But when the man left the king, he went to a fellow servant who owed him a few thousand dollars. He grabbed him by the throat and demanded instant payment.

His fellow servant fell down before him and begged for a little more time. "Be patient with me, and I will pay it," he pleaded. But his creditor wouldn't wait. He had the man arrested and put in prison until the debt could be paid in full.

When some of the other servants saw this, they were very upset. They went to the king and told him everything that had happened. Then the king called in the man he had forgiven and said, "You evil servant! I forgave you that tremendous debt because you pleaded with me. Shouldn't you have mercy on your fellow servant, just as I had mercy on you?" Then the angry king sent the man to prison to be tortured until he had paid his entire debt.

That's what my heavenly Father will do to you if you refuse to forgive your brothers and sisters from your heart.[21]

Some versions of the Bible have a more literal translation of the phrase "sent the man to prison to be tortured." One version reads "delivered him to the jailers,"[22] an older one "delivered him to the *tormentors* (emphasis mine)."[23]

---

21 Matthew 18:23-35 (NLT)
22 NIV85
23 KJV

In Greek—the language of the New Testament—the word for "tormentors" is the same word used for "jailers." If you were in jail, you could count on being tormented. The concept of debtor's prison was simple. If conditions were harsh enough, the debtor would plead with family and friends to supply the necessary funds to cover the debt, thereby gaining his release from the torment.

I don't believe for a moment that our heavenly Father willingly inflicts torment upon people who hold unforgiveness. Rather, He turns us over to the resulting inner turmoil that takes root as offense turns to resentment. The natural conclusion of holding unforgiveness yields the unintended fruit of creating a prison of our own making.

When you hold and nurture resentment over an offense, you become bound to that person or condition by an emotional link that is stronger than steel. Thoughts of *"How could they do this to me?"* morph into imaginary scenarios of what *you* would like to do to them. The more you reflect on the offense—no matter how slight or severe—the deeper the root of bitterness grows. Just the thought of seeing your offender causes you distress. So you begin to script your days in order to minimize the possibility of any encounter with them. "Without forgiveness life is governed by an endless cycle of resentment and retaliation."[24]

As you hold onto unforgiveness, the embittered self begins to construct attitudes and life strategies we call *inner vows*. An inner vow is like a rudder. It sets the course for future relationships and decision making. Self-determining phrases like *I will never trust another man*, or *I will never again let anyone know what I really think* seem likely to provide an emotional buffer zone for our safety.

Instead, these inner vows become building blocks that wall off our hearts from others. One by one they create a barrier to healthy emotional and spiritual relationships. Left long enough, they can become an impenetrable fortress, blocking out people who

24 Roberto Assagioli, http://www.psychologytoday.com/blog/here-there-and-everywhere/201102

love us—and God. We are sucked into the vortex of a tormenting whirlpool. Emotional distress, loneliness, distrust, anger and hatred do their best to drown us in a sea of negativity. A host of physical maladies may begin to appear. Sleeplessness, anxiety, indigestion, arthritis. Any or all of these could be precipitated or worsened if we fail to resolve unforgiveness issues. As long as we don't forgive, whoever or whatever it is will occupy a rent-free space in our mind.[25]

Just like Mrs. Willoughby, we end up injuring ourselves and cutting ourselves off. We imprison *ourselves* in the torment of a living hell. Whenever we continue to live in the state of unforgiveness, we are the ones who suffer—not the person who injured or offended us. Jesus came to set us free. But it is impossible to enjoy the glorious freedom of the children of God while still carrying the weight of bitterness and unforgiveness in your heart.

MAKING THE IMPOSSIBLE POSSIBLE

You might be thinking, *That's a great concept, Harvey. But if you only knew what I've been through, you'd understand why it's impossible for me to forgive.*

Jesus never minimized our pain or hurtful experiences. He experienced life with all of its heartache, grief, and disappointment. "… We do not have a high priest who is unable to sympathize with our weaknesses, but we have one who has been tempted in every way, just as we are—yet was without sin."[26]

He knows our pain. "Surely he has borne our griefs and carried our sorrows; …"[27]

Jesus' teachings must be understood as more than just platitudes or codes of behavior. They are real-life statements of what we *can* do—and will do—when He indwells us. When Jesus made the statement that we are to forgive our brother 490 times, he never expected us to do that simply by the strength of our inner

25 Isabelle Holland, ibid.
26 Hebrews 4:15 (NIV84)
27 Isaiah 53:4a (ESV)

resolve to follow him. He made such a statement knowing that we could only fulfill it by yielding ourselves to him, and letting His Spirit—the Holy Spirit who would live inside of us—empower us to live in obedience to his teachings. His presence within us is the only thing that can give us the capability to live this kind of life.

Forgiving doesn't mean forgetting, nor does it mean that you're sending the message that what someone did was okay. It means that through the grace of God you've let go of the anger or resentment towards someone, or towards yourself. But that can be easier said than done. If forgiveness were easy, everyone would be doing it.[28] Forgiveness doesn't excuse their behavior. Forgiveness prevents their behavior from destroying your heart.

The Christian life was never intended to be lived in our own strength. God's eternal plan was to live inside of us through faith. Then by his indwelling presence, he would be the one to give us the ability to say—just as he did—"Father, forgive them ...."[29]

BREAKING THE POWER

The gateway to forgiveness is not the repentance of the person who offended you. Real forgiveness isn't colored with expectations that the other person apologize—or change. The person you need to forgive may not even be aware of the hurt they caused. Or, if they are, they may not even care.

Forgiveness from the heart comes with no preconditions. No ifs. No fine print. As the saying goes, forgiveness is my giving up the right to hurt you for hurting me.

"We are to forgive so that we may enjoy God's goodness without feeling the weight of anger burning deep within our hearts. Forgiveness does not mean we recant the fact that what happened

---

28 Stephanie Sarkis, PhD., *Here, There and Everywhere*, http://www. psychologytoday.com/blog/here-there-and-everywhere/201102
29 Luke 23:24 (KJV)

24

to us was wrong. Instead, we roll our burdens onto the Lord and allow Him to carry them for us."[30]

Forgiveness does not change the past. It frees us from the tyranny of being controlled by it.

For over two centuries, the first song in the book of hymns of the Methodist Church has been "O for a thousand tongues to sing." The words of the fourth stanza mirror the dramatic change in the life of hymn writer Charles Wesley.

> He breaks the power of canceled sin,
> He sets the prisoner free;
> His blood can make the foulest clean,
> His blood availed for me.

I have always thought of *breaking the power of canceled sin* in two ways. The first is in regard to my own sin. It is absolutely true that the cross of Christ settled once and for all everything that needed to be done to atone for our sins. Sin's power was canceled at Calvary. But having the application of this forgiveness in my life—the breaking of the power of sin—only happened at the time that I accepted Christ. Once I knew Him, the sin canceled on Calvary could no longer accuse and condemn me. The power of sin was broken and no longer could hold me in bondage.

The second way to think about *breaking the power of canceled sin* is in breaking the power of others' sins against *me*. I might remember the events and the specific occurrence of the offense, but that memory—and its power to control my thoughts and actions—no longer can exert any influence over my life. "Forgiving does not erase the bitter past. A healed memory is not a deleted memory. Instead, forgiving what we cannot forget creates a new

30 Charles Stanley, *Landmines in the Path of the Believer*, http://christianity.about.com/od/topicaldevotions

way to remember. We change the memory of our past into a hope for our future."[31]

As Lewis Smedes says, "When you release the wrongdoer from the wrong, you cut a malignant tumor out of your inner life. You set a prisoner free, but you discover that the real prisoner was yourself."[32]

31 Lewis Smedes, http://www.psychologytoday.com/blog/here-there-and-everywhere/201102/
32 Lewis B. Smedes, *Forgive and Forget*, http://christianity.about.com/od/topicaldevotions/ss/Forgiveness-Quotes_7.htm

FORGIVENESS QUESTIONS AND ANSWERS

Question: *I have done some really bad things in my life. Will God forgive me?*

Answer: Yes, God will forgive you. His forgiveness extends to each of us regardless of what we have done. The apostle Paul gives a list of some "bad" sins that people commit. Then he goes on to declare that although some of us were like this, we have been forgiven—clearly an example of the breadth of God's forgiveness. "Do not be deceived: Neither the sexually immoral nor idolaters nor adulterers nor men who have sex with men nor thieves nor the greedy nor drunkards nor slanderers nor swindlers will inherit the kingdom of God. And that is what some of you were (emphasis mine). But you were washed, you were sanctified, you were justified in the name of the Lord Jesus Christ and by the Spirit of our God" (1 Corinthians 6:9-11 NIV). This portion of scripture covers some pretty bad stuff, but Paul emphasizes what Jesus does for those who turn to him. This is Good News indeed.

Question: *I asked God to forgive me, but don't feel any different. Am I really forgiven?*

Answer: When it comes to forgiveness, we must understand that the basis for our receiving forgiveness is determined by God himself. We accept his verdict. As the supreme judge of all, his ruling in each case stands. Never refer God's judgments to the lower court of your own opinion. Believe that what God says is true. Therefore, if we confess our sins to him, he *is* faithful and just to forgive our sins, and cleanse us from all unrighteousness (1 John 1:9). Your feelings of forgiveness may not be immediate. But forgiveness is based on God's *facts*, not your *feelings*. Give it a little time. Keep thanking the Lord for forgiving you. Eventually your feelings will catch up with His reality.

Question: *I really want to live for God, but I keep committing the same sin over and over. I'm worried that God will get fed up with me and quit forgiving me. Will He?*

Answer: You need to know that you are not alone in this challenge. Being stuck in a pattern of repetitive sin is a huge issue for many Christians (I know from my own experience). Please hear me very clearly. There is *no limit* to the grace of God. Obviously it's wrong to live a life of careless rebellion and tell yourself, "It doesn't matter what I do. God will forgive me." Your asking this question indicates to me that you clearly want to please God. But you feel powerless to live victoriously over this particular sin. Whenever you come to the Lord with an humble and repentant heart and ask for forgiveness, you receive it because of Christ's death, burial, and resurrection. Forgiveness is based on *his* faithfulness, not ours.

I want to encourage you. God's power extends far beyond forgiveness. Jude (the brother of Jesus) tells us that "… [he] is able to *keep you from falling* and to present you before his glorious presence *without fault* and with great joy."[33] It is a lie from the Enemy that you are going to have to live all your life stuck in sinful patterns of behavior. God can—and will—through the power of his indwelling Holy Spirit, give you the strength to resist temptation and overcome sin. Many of the repetitive sins we become slaves to are the result of trying to deal with legitimate needs in illegitimate ways. We use drugs or alcohol or sex or any other number of things to try to ease hurt or emotional pain in our lives. Just like Satan's lie to Eve (about the benefits of disobeying God and eating the fruit), it doesn't make things better—only worse. We end up enslaved. But take heart. Jesus came to set captives free.

From my own experience (and from the experience of countless others), an open confession of our sin to another person has been instrumental in helping us to walk free from besetting sins. By open confession, I mean finding a trusted pastor, counselor, or mature Christian friend to whom you can confess the sins you've committed. I don't suggest going into gory detail, but sharing briefly the nature of the struggle and your desire to be free. Then have them pray over you prayers of forgiveness and restoration. James

---

33 Jude 24 (NIV84)

5:16 addresses this: "Confess your sins to each other and pray for each other so that you may be healed. The earnest prayer of a righteous person has great power and produces wonderful results" (NLT).

You also need to grow in discipleship. A person who struggles with repetitive sin frequently does so for years. Don't be surprised if takes time to learn to live in victory. You may well receive instant and lasting freedom through prayer. But you still need to learn how to walk in your new-found freedom. Years of patterning will take time to change. There are some terrific resources available to help you. Your pastor or counselor can assist you in this area.

Question: *I have asked someone to forgive me for something I did to them. They said OK, but keep bringing it back up whenever we are together. What should I do?*

Answer: If the person keeps bringing this up, they clearly have not been able to forgive and move on from their hurt. You cannot be responsible for their spiritual and emotional health. You are only responsible for yourself. If you have truly repented and confessed to them, there is no more that you can do. If they bring it up again, it's OK to say something like, "You know that I have asked you to forgive me, and you said yes. But bringing it up repeatedly makes me think you still have issues with me. I know that I can't undo what's been done. If I could, I would. Do you think you can let it go?" If they can, good. If not, you may need to keep some emotional distance from the person for your own well-being. Just keep asking the Lord to love that person through you. Keep praying for them. And leave the results to God.

Question: *I have tried to truly forgive somebody who hurt me deeply. How do I know if I really have?*

Answer: A good test is how you would feel if you see that person. If the thought of such an encounter makes you uncomfortable, that may be an indication that there's more work to be done. Depending on the severity of the offense, you may need to seek a

Christian counselor or pastor who can help you find healing from the heart wounds that accompanied the offense.

Question: *I have heard that there is an unpardonable sin, and I am afraid I have committed it. Can you help?*

Answer: Jesus' mention of a sin that would not be pardoned is in Mark 3:28-30, "I tell you the truth, all the sins and blasphemies of men will be forgiven them. But whoever blasphemes against the Holy Spirit will never be forgiven; he is guilty of an eternal sin." He said this because they were saying, "He has an evil spirit."[34]

In this section of scripture, some were saying that Jesus had power over evil spirits because he himself had demons! The important part to note are Jesus' words, "I tell you the truth, all the sins and blasphemies of men will be forgiven them." Since you are not accusing Jesus of being demon possessed, you have no worry about having committed an unpardonable sin. I think that the devil is using this false accusation to keep you in fear and doubt. Remember, if we confess our sins to him, he is faithful and just to forgive us.

---

34 (NIV84)

Forgiveness Scriptures

The following list of scripture verses are taken from the New International Version, 1984 Edition. For easier reference, the list is separated into Old and New Testament. These are not all the scriptures pertaining to forgiveness but a significant sampling of those pertinent to this book. I encourage you to look them up in your Bible, and commit some to memory.

Old Testament

Numbers 14:20 — The Lord replied, "I have forgiven them, as you asked."

2 Chronicles 7:14 — ... if my people, who are called by my name, will humble themselves and pray and seek my face and turn from their wicked ways, then will I hear from heaven and will forgive their sin and will heal their land.

Nehemiah 9:17 — They refused to listen and failed to remember the miracles you performed among them. They became stiff-necked and in their rebellion appointed a leader in order to return to their slavery. But you are a forgiving God, gracious and compassionate, slow to anger and abounding in love. Therefore you did not desert them.

Psalm 32:1-2b — Blessed is he whose transgressions are forgiven, whose sins are covered. Blessed is the man whose sin the Lord does not count against him ...

Psalm 32:5 — Then I acknowledged my sin to you and did not cover up my iniquity. I said, "I will confess my transgressions to the Lord"— and you forgave the guilt of my sin.

Psalm 65:3 — When we were overwhelmed by sins, you forgave our transgressions.

Psalm 78:38 — Yet he was merciful; he forgave their iniquities and did not destroy them. Time after time he restrained his anger and did not stir up his full wrath.

Psalm 85:2 — You forgave the iniquity of your people and covered all their sins.

Psalm 86:5 — You are forgiving and good, O Lord, abounding in love to all who call to you.

Psalm 99:8 — O Lord our God, you answered them; you were to Israel a forgiving God, though you punished their misdeeds.

Psalm 103:3 — … who forgives all your sins and heals all your diseases,

Psalm 130:4 — But with you there is forgiveness; therefore you are feared.

Isaiah 38:17b — In your love you kept me from the pit of destruction; you have put all my sins behind your back.

Isaiah 43:25 — I, even I, and he who blots out your transgressions, for my own sake, and remembers your sins no more.

Isaiah 44:22 — I have swept away your offenses like a cloud, your sins like the morning mist. Return to me, for I have redeemed you.

Jeremiah 31:34 — No longer will a man teach his neighbor, or a man his brother, saying, 'Know the Lord,' because they will all know me, from the least of them to the greatest," declares the Lord. "For I will forgive their wickedness and will remember their sins no more."

Jeremiah 33:8 — I will cleanse them from all the sin they have committed against me and will forgive all their sins of rebellion against me.

Jeremiah 50:20 — In those days, at that time," declares the Lord, "search will be made for Israel's guilt, but there will be none, and for the sins of Judah, but none will be found, for I will forgive the remnant I spare.

Daniel 9:9 — The Lord our God is merciful and forgiving, even though we have rebelled against him;

Micah 7:18 — Who is a God like you, who pardons sin and forgives the transgression of the remnant of his inheritance? You do not stay angry forever but delight to show mercy.

NEW TESTAMENT

Matthew 6:12 — Forgive us our debts, as we also have forgiven our debtors.

Matthew 6:14 — For if you forgive men when they sin against you, your heavenly Father will also forgive you.

Matthew 6:15 — But if you do not forgive men their sins, your Father will not forgive your sins.

Matthew 9:2 — Some men brought to him a paralytic, lying on a mat. When Jesus saw their faith, he said to the paralytic, "Take heart, son; your sins are forgiven."

Matthew 9:5 — Which is easier: to say, 'Your sins are forgiven,' or to say, 'Get up and walk'?

Matthew 9:6 — But so that you may know that the Son of Man has authority on earth to forgive sins …." Then he said to the paralytic, "Get up, take your mat and go home."

Matthew 12:31 — And so I tell you, every sin and blasphemy will be forgiven men, but the blasphemy against the Spirit will not be forgiven.

Matthew 12:32 — Anyone who speaks a word against the Son of Man will be forgiven, but anyone who speaks against the Holy Spirit will not be forgiven, either in this age or in the age to come.

Matthew 26:28 — This is my blood of the covenant, which is poured out for many for the forgiveness of sins.

Mark 2:5 — When Jesus saw their faith, he said to the paralytic, "Son, your sins are forgiven."

Mark 2:7 — "Why does this fellow talk like that? He's blaspheming! Who can forgive sins but God alone?"

Mark 3:28 — I tell you the truth, all the sins and blasphemies of men will be forgiven them.

Mark 11:25 — And when you stand praying, if you hold anything against anyone, forgive him, so that your Father in heaven may forgive you your sins.

Luke 1:77 — ... to give his people the knowledge of salvation through the forgiveness of their sins,

Luke 3:3 — He went into all the country around the Jordan, preaching a baptism of repentance for the forgiveness of sins.

Luke 5:20 — When Jesus saw their faith, he said, "Friend, your sins are forgiven."

Luke 5:21 — The Pharisees and the teachers of the law began thinking to themselves, "Who is this fellow who speaks blasphemy? Who can forgive sins but God alone?"

Luke 5:23 — Which is easier: to say, 'Your sins are forgiven,' or to say, 'Get up and walk'?

Luke 5:24 — "But that you may know that the Son of Man has authority on earth to forgive sins ...." He said to the paralyzed man, "I tell you, get up, take your mat and go home."

Luke 6:37 — Do not judge, and you will not be judged. Do not condemn, and you will not be condemned. Forgive, and you will be forgiven.

Luke 7:47 — Therefore, I tell you, her many sins have been forgiven—for she loved much. But he who has been forgiven little loves little.

Luke 7:48 — Then Jesus said to her, "Your sins are forgiven."

Luke 7:49 — The other guests began to say among themselves, "Who is this who even forgives sins?"

Luke 11:4 — Forgive us our sins, for we also forgive everyone who sins against us. And lead us not into temptation.

Luke 12:10 — And everyone who speaks a word against the Son of Man will be forgiven, but anyone who blasphemes against the Holy Spirit will not be forgiven.

Luke 17:3 — So watch yourselves. If your brother sins, rebuke him, and if he repents, forgive him.

Luke 17:4 — If he sins against you seven times in a day, and seven times comes back to you and says, 'I repent,' forgive him.

Luke 23:34 — Jesus said, "Father, forgive them, for they do not know what they are doing." And they divided up his clothes by casting lots.

Luke 24:47 — … and repentance and forgiveness of sins will be preached in his name to all nations, beginning at Jerusalem.

John 20:23 — If you forgive anyone his sins, they are forgiven; if you do not forgive them, they are not forgiven.

Acts 2:38 — Peter replied, "Repent and be baptized, every one of you, in the name of Jesus Christ for the forgiveness of your sins. And you will receive the gift of the Holy Spirit."

Acts 5:31 — God exalted him to his own right hand as Prince and Savior that he might give repentance and forgiveness of sins to Israel.

Acts 8:22 — Repent of this wickedness and pray to the Lord. Perhaps he will forgive you for having such a thought in your heart.

Acts 10:43 — All the prophets testify about him that everyone who believes in him receives forgiveness of sins through his name.

Acts 13:38 — Therefore, my brothers, I want you to know that through Jesus the forgiveness of sins is proclaimed to you.

Acts 26:18 — … to open their eyes and turn them from darkness to light, and from the power of Satan to God, so that they may receive forgiveness of sins and a place among those who are sanctified by faith in me.

Romans 4:7 — Blessed are they whose transgressions are forgiven, whose sins are covered.

2 Corinthians 2:7 — Now instead, you ought to forgive and comfort him, so that he will not be overwhelmed by excessive sorrow.

2 Corinthians 2:10 — If you forgive anyone, I also forgive him. And what I have forgiven—if there was anything to forgive—I have forgiven in the sight of Christ for your sake, …

2 Corinthians 5:19 — … God was reconciling the world to himself in Christ, not counting men's sins against them …

2 Corinthians 12:13 — How were you inferior to the other churches, except that I was never a burden to you? Forgive me this wrong!

Ephesians 1:7 — In him we have redemption through his blood, the forgiveness of sins, in accordance with the riches of God's grace

Ephesians 4:32 — Be kind and compassionate to one another, forgiving each other, just as in Christ God forgave you.

Colossians 1:14 — ... in whom we have redemption, the forgiveness of sins.

Colossians 2:13 — When you were dead in your sins and in the uncircumcision of your sinful nature, God made you alive with Christ. He forgave us all our sins,

Colossians 3:13 — Bear with each other and forgive whatever grievances you may have against one another. Forgive as the Lord forgave you.

Hebrews 8:12 — For I will forgive their wickedness and will remember their sins no more.

Hebrews 9:22 — In fact, the law requires that nearly everything be cleansed with blood, and without the shedding of blood there is no forgiveness.

Hebrews 10:18 — And where these have been forgiven, there is no longer any sacrifice for sin.

James 5:15 — And the prayer offered in faith will make the sick person well; the Lord will raise him up. If he has sinned, he will be forgiven.

1 John 1:9 — If we confess our sins, he is faithful and just and will forgive us our sins and purify us from all unrighteousness.

1 John 2:12 — I write to you, dear children, because your sins have been forgiven on account of his name.

ABOUT THE AUTHOR

Dr. Harvey R. Brown, Jr. is President of Impact Ministries, Inc. in Pigeon Forge, Tennessee. You can find out more about him by visiting his website: www.impactministries.org